ON CAMERA

THE STORY OF
A CHILD ACTOR

by
JOAN HEWETT

photographs by
RICHARD HEWETT

Clarion Books
New York

For Christopher, Angela, and Jonathan

Clarion Books
a Houghton Mifflin Company imprint
215 Park Avenue South, New York, NY 10003
Text copyright © 1987 by Joan Hewett
Photographs copyright © 1987 by Richard Hewett

Printed in Italy
Library of Congress Cataloging-in-Publication Data
Hewett, Joan.
   On camera.

   Summary: Text and photographs present a close-up view
of the life of eight-year-old child actor Philip Waller
as he goes to auditions, makes commercials, and films a
television special.
   1. Waller, Philip—Juvenile literature. 2. Actors—
United States—Biography—Juvenile literature.
3. Children as actors—United States—Juvenile literature.
[1. Waller, Philip. 2. Actors and actresses.
3. Children as actors] I. Hewett, Richard, ill.
II. Title.
PN2287.W34H4 1987   792'.028'09 [B] [92]   87-5125
ISBN 0-89919-469-9   PA ISBN 0-395-54788-1

NWI 10 9 8 7 6 5 4 3 2 1

Philip Waller mounts the bare stage. "Who are you? Where are you?" his drama coach, Diane Hardin, asks.

Philip thinks about the person he's pretending to be. He tries to feel what the person feels. Then he looks out into the dark studio toward his classmates.

Tonight is Philip's weekly acting class at Young Actors Space. The studio, which is run by actress Diane Hardin, is in California's San Fernando Valley, close to film and video production companies and major movie and TV studios. Many of the children and young people who study here are professional actors. They appear in TV commercials, TV series and features, and in theatrical films—movies that are shown in theaters.

Eight-year-old Philip has been acting for almost two years. He has appeared in fourteen TV commercials and has had small roles in a couple of TV dramas.

"I'm lucky," Philip says. "I love to act, and I'm learning to do something that I might be able to do when I'm grown-up. Of course, by then I may have decided to be a marine biologist. I don't know. But right now acting is number one."

Actors use their bodies and voices to perform, so they must learn to use them well. At Young Actors Space, the sessions begin with warm-up exercises.

"Bend," the drama coach says. "Put your head down. Let it go. Let it go, like an apple on a branch. Roll your head up. Now you're really mean. Really happy. Shoulders up. Shoulders down. Up and down, move them around."

Next come the voice exercises. First the students in the class hum together. Their *h-u-m-z-z-s* buzz and swell.

They follow that with tongue twisters.

"Butter gutter, noodle poodle, giggle gaggle....Any noise annoys an oyster, but a noisy noise annoys an oyster most."

Then Diane announces that the skits and scenes will begin. Most of the skits are improvisational. Coach or students suggest a plot, then the actors make up the lines as they go along. This trains the students to "live in the moment," to watch, listen, and respond to one another.

Natalie Strahl

Eric Ratican

CHRISTIE CLARK
Twentieth Century Artists, Inc.

JENNIFER
ROOSENDAHL

Sharon
Smith

Twentieth Century Artists, Inc.

Heather Martin
Hair: Brown / Eyes: Blue
Date of Birth: 9/28/78

Toni Kelman & Associates

GINA-MARIE
LANDON

Sometimes the students are divided into acting teams. Each team is given its opening lines and has five minutes or so to come up with a plot. If the studio's rehearsal rooms are occupied by other classes, the teams huddle in a corridor to plan their scenes. The wall of the corridor is lined with their composites: photographs of themselves with their name as well as the name and phone number of the agent who represents them.

Tonight, after the skits are over, Philip's acting group gets to perform with the older students. They do scenes from well-known plays. Philip is paired with Crista Denton, who has had leading roles in TV movies.

"Crista's a really good actress," Philip says. "When we perform together, I try extra hard."

All too soon the scene ends, the three hour class is over, and it is time for Philip to go home.

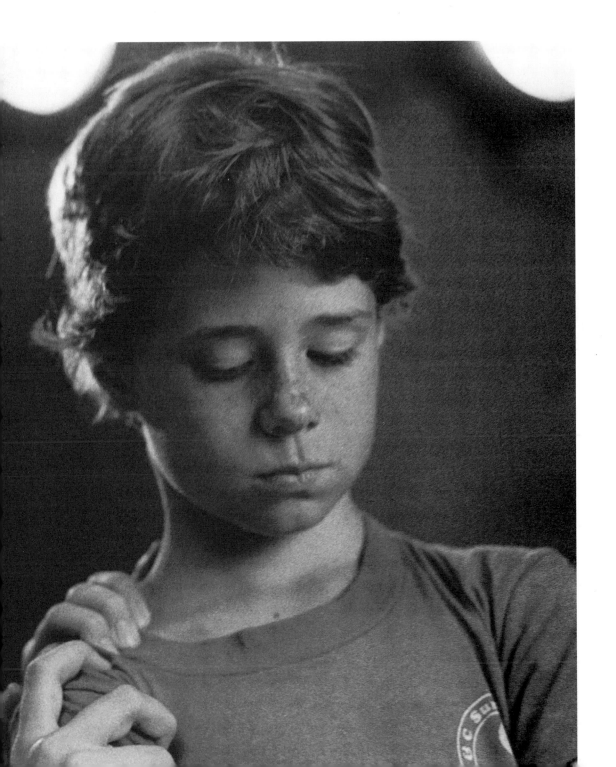

Philip is in the third grade. When he's not on camera, he goes to school from 9:00 A.M. to 3:00 P.M. Like most actors, he gets cast for parts by auditioning, trying out for them. Under California law, auditions for young people must be held after 3:00 P.M. so that children have a full day in school.

"Auditioning can be fun," Philip says, "especially when you're given your 'sides,' pages from a script, ahead of time and you get to act! There are loads of parts for children in TV commercials. I don't get most of the parts I try out for. But I don't worry about it now. I do my best, and I hope that the casting director remembers me. Maybe I'll be right for the next commercial."

This afternoon Philip is auditioning for a children's vitamin commercial. His mother, Kathy Waller, is taking him, and his sisters, six-year-old Maria and two-year-old Nicole, come along. When they reach the building, Philip rushes in. His appointment is for 3:40 P.M. He is just on time!

Philip signs the union sign-in sheet and enters the time. When he leaves, he'll enter that time as well. Sign-in sheets are a record of who has been to an audition and for how long. According to the actors' unions that regulate film and TV auditions, actors who have to wait more than an hour must be paid "waiting time."

An assistant is collecting composites. Philip hands his over. Then he looks at the other children and decides that there must be more than one "spot," or opening, for an actor in the commercial.

Philip is right. There are four parts for children in the commercial, and the casting director is looking for children for each one. She has called agents who represent child actors and described by physical appearance and personality the type of actors she is looking for. From the composites she received, she selected about one hundred children. Starting today, she will be interviewing them. Each interview will be videotaped so it can be viewed again. Finally the casting director will decide which of these young actors are good possibilities. They will receive a "call-back," a request to return for another audition.

As one child leaves the audition room, the next child is asked in. Soon it is Philip's turn.

The casting director is friendly and direct. She tells Philip her name and shows him where to stand. Philip "slates," he looks into the camera and gives his name and age. Then the casting director asks where he goes to school and what grade he is in.

"What's your favorite subject?" she asks next.

"English," Philip says, "because I like to read."

"What's your favorite book?"

Philip thinks of the books he's read recently. Then he comes up with his all-time favorite, *Where the Wild Things Are.*

The casting director switches the subject. "Do you like sports? Are you on a team?"

Philip's eyes sparkle. He loves to play soccer. He tells her about his team, the team he was on last fall. Then at her request, he stretches high. After that he pretends to pick up something heavy, so heavy he can hardly lift it. Finally the casting director smiles and says, "Thank you very much."

The audition has taken less than five minutes. Philip's agents will let him know if he receives a call-back.

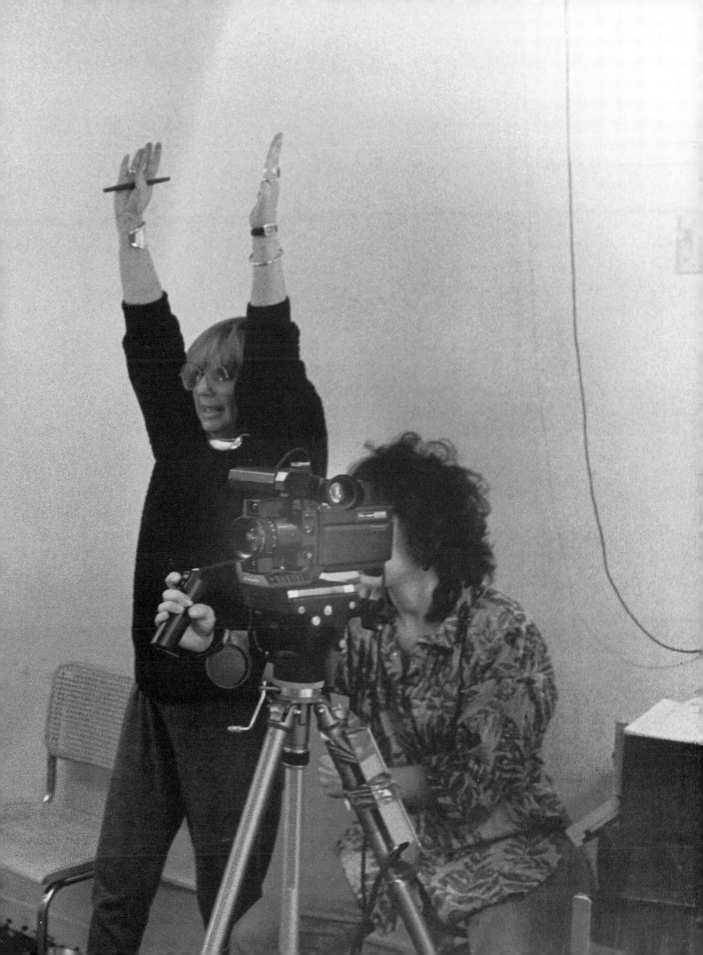

As the Wallers head homeward, Kathy suggests stopping off to see Philip's agents, Twentieth Century Artists, Inc. The agency represents children and young people exclusively. Vivian Hollander and Estelle Hertzberg, the owner-manager team, encourage their youthful actors to drop in from time to time. Estelle asks Philip how the vitamin commercial went, and Vivian quickly measures him to see if he has grown. Then she opens her notebook to Philip's page.

Both agents have notebooks that list each actor's name, date of birth, and his or her physical description and professional credits—acting jobs. New credits are continually added, and so, occasionally, is a youngster's height.

Telephones ring steadily in an agent's office. A casting director will call and say, "I have two spots. I need—" and the agent takes down the information. The term "slight character type" is often used. It means an actor who is attractive with an appealing, slightly offbeat personality. Child actors like Philip who are slight character types are more in demand than children who are beautiful or handsome. When the call ends, the agent looks through her notebook for actors who fit the description. Then their composites are pulled from the file and sent by messenger to the casting director.

Sometimes a casting director requests a certain actor, and sometimes agents suggest and "talk up" a specific actor or actors. Agents receive a percentage of what each of their actors earn, so agents want each actor to be as successful as possible.

Philip dreams of getting a big role in a TV movie or special. He wants to be able to create a part and really act, like he does at Young Actors Space. Twice his hopes were high. Then each time, after several call-backs, he lost to the competing actor. Estelle and Vivian believe that Philip will succeed. They know that he has the needed determination. They think that he has the talent, and they will continue to suggest him for dramatic roles.

When the Wallers get home, Philip plays outside for fifteen minutes before starting on his homework. Then after dinner he returns to his room to finish it.

Philip's dad, Howard, designs computer programs. He has taped most of Philip's commercials, and while Philip is studying, the family decides to watch them again. When Philip joins his family, he's amazed. He looks so small in his first commercial, but it doesn't seem that long ago. He can remember clearly how it all began.

He had been watching Saturday morning cartoons on TV, but it was the commercials that had sparked his imagination. The children in them seemed to be having so much fun! I could do that...he thought.

"Philip Waller, you're only six and a half years old," his mom had said when they'd talked about it. His dad hadn't thought much of the idea either. But his parents did think that he might enjoy acting: he was a natural mimic, had nonstop energy, and a lively imagination. So they enrolled him in Le Petit Repertory Theatre, a local children's theater group that puts on plays.

Philip did enjoy acting. But the more he performed on stage, the more he wanted to perform on camera. After a few months, his parents agreed to give him the chance. His mom planned to call SAG, the Screen Actors Guild, for names of agents. She was going to send a photo of Philip to the agent and request an interview. But before she could follow through, a Twentieth Century Artist talent scout came to a play at Le Petit Repertory Theatre. She spotted Philip and set up an interview at the agency.

"I could hardly sit still," Philip recalls. "Vivian and Estelle asked me questions about myself and why I wanted to be in commercials. Then they called my mom in. They talked about the cost of photos and having composites made and how much of a mom's time her child's career might take. I got sort of worried, but my mom kept nodding and saying yes.

"When I was accepted by the agency, I thought—now there's no stopping me. I went to a couple of auditions, and I paid extra attention in school. I wanted to be ready." To work in California, minors need permits, and for school-age children this means a report card that shows good grades and satisfactory conduct.

Philip auditioned week after week. First he was over-confident, he thought he would get every part. But nothing happened, and he began to feel like a failure. Vivian and Estelle thought he was trying too hard. They told him to relax, to be himself. After two months of auditioning, he got his first call-back! Then on his twenty-sixth tryout, he made it. He got the part!

Now Philip could get his work permit and his SAG card.

The commercial took three days to make. It was shot partly in a studio and partly on location, and Philip had the leading part!

In a few weeks Philip landed a part in another commercial. After a slow start he was on his way.

Although Philip is very busy now, he still loves to take part in the plays at Le Petit Repertory Theatre.

"It's fun," Philip says. "You wear crazy costumes, and there's singing and dancing. I like that. When you're doing a TV commercial, everything has to be perfect. Each filming of a scene is called a 'take,' and sometimes there are twenty or thirty takes! Also you don't do the scenes in their real order. But when you're performing on the stage, you start at the beginning and you go all the way through to the end. At Le Petit Repertory, no one minds if a performance doesn't go quite as well as it could. The children in the audience are having a good time, and so do you."

The company puts on two plays a season, and each

play runs several times. Everyone gets to be in every play. *Alice in Wonderland* was the first play in the spring season. The second play is *The Wizard of Oz*, and Philip is the Tin Man. It's the best part in the whole play, Philip decides as the applause fades. And then he has second thoughts—it might be fun to be the Wizard.

A new school week begins, and Philip is looking forward to his school field trip on Thursday. His class is going hiking in the mountains, and they'll visit a wild animal sanctuary. His field trip permission slip was signed weeks ago, and the day marked off on the calendar. But Monday afternoon, Philip learns that his upcoming TV commercial has been moved to Thursday.

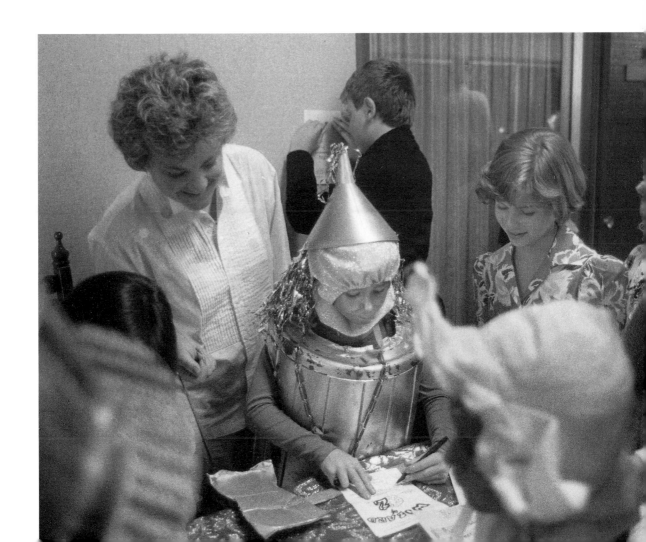

"They can't do that," Philip tells his mom. "I won't be in the commercial. Maybe if they know that I won't, they'll change the day." His mom gives him a long look. "Well, it's not fair," Philip says.

Philip feels sorry for himself for quite a while. The night before a commercial Howard helps Philip rehearse. He reads the lines of all the other actors, so Philip can memorize his cues—the words or actions that prompt Philip's words or actions. Philip starts—almost against his will—to wonder what the set will look like. The next morning he's dressed early and ready to go.

At the studio gate, Philip's mom gives the guard Philip's name. The guard checks his list and says, "Oh, yes, Philip Waller." Philip tries to look casual, but he feels sort of important. The guard tells them where to park and directs them to Sound Stage Three. Once again, Philip finds a studio backlot an exciting, even mysterious, place to be. Maybe some of the barnlike sound stages are deserted. Maybe movies or TV shows are being filmed inside.

On Sound Stage Three, grips are moving equipment and gaffers are just beginning to light the set. Other people, off to one side, are talking or drinking coffee. When the Wallers enter, Philip's teacher—welfare worker introduces herself. In accordance with California law, she will be there as long as he is. Together with Kathy, she will be overseeing Philip's welfare. She will also spend three hours with Philip instructing him in his regular schoolwork. Now Philip goes along with her to the classroom.

In an off-the-set classroom, lessons are planned around the shooting schedule, so some are long and others are short. "I work harder than I do in school," Philip says. "I concentrate. I don't want to be behind when I go back."

As Philip finishes memorizing a multiplication table, there's a knock on the door. "I'm just going to put cheeks on you," the makeup woman says.

"Philip!" a production assistant calls. The director is almost ready to shoot. Philip takes his place beside another actor in a mock-up of a helicopter's interior. They are supposed to be flying past the Statue of Liberty in New York Harbor, and when the scene is completed, it will look as if they are! The director and his crew filmed the statue in New York weeks ago. By using a process called "blue screen," that filmed footage will be added electronically to the footage they are about to shoot.

Now Philip looks out the helicopter window toward the blank backdrop. He finds his eyeline, an off-camera mark that shows where Miss Liberty's face will be.

"Take One," a production assistant says.

"Okay, roll 'em," the director says.

Philip pretends to see the famed statue. "Oh, Grandpa, she's beautiful!" he exclaims in a voice filled with awe and delight.

Later in the day the same scene is shot from another point of view. Instead of the camera looking across the actors and out the window, the camera now looks through the window at the actors.

The shooting is over, and as he and his mom drive home, Philip looks forward to a swim in the family pool. But it is dark when they arrive at the house, and the water is cold. Fortunately, Saturday is warm and sunny. Philip dives in and swims the length of the pool underwater while his dad relaxes in the sun.

"Will you teach me to surf this summer?" Philip asks Howard.

"Not this summer," Howard says.

"I'll be nine soon; that's pretty old. And once school is out, I'll have lots of free time."

Howard tells him that he might enjoy some free time.

"I don't think so," Philip replies.

Philip is just as busy as ever during the next few weeks. There is school, Monday night judo lessons, his Wednesday night actors' workshop, stage rehearsals and performances at Le Petit Repertory Theatre, family activities, and TV work. Howard and Kathy decide that Philip should slow down. After some objections from Philip, an agreement is reached. From now on Philip will spend only two afternoons a week going to auditions instead of three or four. But if he gets a call for a big dramatic part, he'll go for it, regardless.

That special call doesn't come, so Philip just enjoys two TV jobs. One is a very small acting part in a TV soap, a daytime serial. The other part is in a TV commercial. The commercial seems more like play than work. It is shot on location in the city, his part is easy, and five other children who are about his own age are in it.

When a TV commercial is filmed, the actors who appear in it are paid "scale," a minimum union rate for each day they work. Then later on when the commercial runs on TV the actors' earnings increase. They earn a small sum known as a residual each time it is shown. The size of the residual is based on the estimated number of people who see the commercial.

The money that Philip has earned has been saved for his college education. "I'm going to be able to pay for most, or maybe even all, of my college tuition!" Philip says. "I'm proud of that."

A few weeks go by. Then one afternoon when Philip is supposed to walk home from school, his mom's car is right outside. Even her eyes seem to be smiling at him as he approaches. When he gets in the car, she hands him a script. A TV special based on Beverly Cleary's book *The Mouse and the Motorcycle* is going to be made, and Philip is up for the human lead, a boy named Keith!

"When do I try out?" Philip asks.

"In about an hour," Kathy replies, and although she explains that the director simply wants him to be familiar with his character, Philip panics. He's cold; his hands sweat. Then as he reads, he gets caught up in the story. And by the time they arrive, he's eager, a little scared, and also kind of confident.

"I'll be Ralph the mouse," Ron Underwood, the director, says. Philip slates for the video camera. Then the director tells him the page and scene number and starts reading. Philip finds the scene easy to imagine. He thinks what fun it would be to stop at a creaky old hotel and discover a talking mouse—particularly a mouse who loves motorcycles! As he reads Keith's lines, Philip can almost feel what Keith feels.

"That was nice," the director says when they come to the end of the scene. Philip is curious... is Ralph going to be a mechanical mouse or a trained mouse?

The director explains that there will be more than one Ralph. The Ralph whom Keith befriends will be a mechanical, cable-operated puppet. Then he suggests that they read another couple of scenes. "You're still Keith, and I'll take all the other parts. Okay?"

Philip is delighted. "Okay."

"That was very nice, Philip," the director says when they finish. "Now what I'd like you to do is take your script home. Read it, think about it, memorize the first scene that we read, and come back again tomorrow."

The next day no video camera intrudes as the director and Philip speak and react to each other. Sometimes they try a scene more than one way. Sometimes the director suggests that Philip say a line differently.

When the audition ends, the director thanks Philip politely. Philip hesitates—he knows he read well, and he wants the part so much. He looks at Ron for some sign... but Ron turns away, and Philip walks to the reception room where his mom and Nicole wait.

For months, Ron Underwood has been looking for a child to play Keith. Because the role is so important, Ron had at first limited the auditions to child actors who had already played leading roles in films or TV features.

"Some of the youngsters read well," the director said, "but I never said to myself, 'that's Keith.' So I kept on looking. Philip's first reading was outstanding. He talked to Ralph naturally. He sounded like he was speaking to a surprising and unusual but real mouse. Then when Philip read again, he showed that he was flexible and could take direction."

But Ron is still not sure. Philip has talent. He also looks right for the part. But does he have staying power? They will be filming for two weeks. The part is long, and the scenes won't be shot in sequence. Some scenes will have to be done over and over. Will Philip's energy hold? Will he be able to concentrate his efforts?

Filming starts on Monday. Ron must decide.

The next afternoon Philip gets a call from one of his agents. She's just received word. The part is his!

Philip rehearses with Ron on Friday afternoon and again on Saturday. Ron shows him the *Mouse and the Motorcycle* storyboard: a series of drawings that show each scene from the camera's point of view. The director explains that the storyboard will be on the set so the cameraman will be able to see how each upcoming scene should be shot. Then he smiles and puts his arm around Philip. "See you Monday morning on the set."

"Wait, don't leave without this," the assistant producer calls to Philip. She hands him his shooting schedule for the first week. The schedule lists by day and date the "cast calls," the time the actors are due on the set and the scenes that will be shot. Most of the script will be filmed on a sound stage that is about an hour's drive from Los Angeles, so a freeway map and instructions are attached.

Monday morning Philip is excited and nervous as he and his mom drive along. When they pull into the parking lot, no people are around and all the buildings are unmarked. Philip wonders if they are in the wrong place.

"Good morning!" the assistant producer calls cheerfully as they get out of the car. Philip rushes through the open door. His first-morning jitters are almost gone as he walks out onto the sound stage.

It seems enormous! But the hotel bedroom where he discovers Ralph looks small and somehow odd. Philip walks closer. Why, of course! The set is built on a platform several feet off the floor. He peers underneath.

"Nothing's there yet," Ron says. Then he explains that the mouse's controls will be on the floor underneath the mouse hole. The special effects director, the man who designed all the Ralphs, will be sitting under the set operating the controls.

46

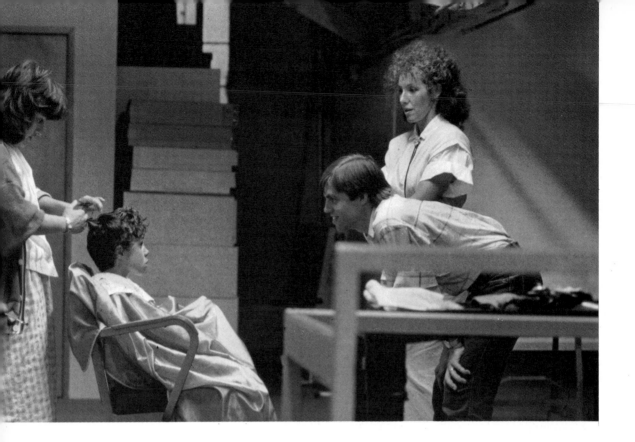

Soon it is time for Philip to have his haircut. School-work comes next. Although Philip tries, he can barely keep his mind on what he is reading. An hour passes before he is called to wardrobe.

While the cameraman and the assistant cameraman were lining up their shot and the gaffers were adjusting and readjusting their lights, Philip's stand-in, a boy about Philip's age, was taking Philip's place. Now as Philip comes on the set, his stand-in leaves. The boys say hi to each other, and the stand-in heads for the classroom.

Ron shows Philip his "mark," the spot where he is to stand. He talks to him about the upcoming scene, and they go over the first few lines.

Then Ron says, "All right." And the assistant director says, "Bell, please."

The bell rings, signaling for everyone to be quiet. At the same time, the red—warning stay out—light by the outside sound stage door goes on. No one may enter until the light is turned off.

"Camera," the assistant director says.

"Rolling," the cameraman replies.

"Sound," the assistant director says.

"Speed," the sound mixer replies, telling the assistant director that the sound is going at the proper rate of speed.

"Mark," the assistant director says.

A member of the crew places a clapboard (hinged sticks, attached to a chalkboard) before the camera and says, "Scene One. Take One." Then he strikes the clapper closed. The sound will be synchronized with the image, so the sound and film will start at the same moment.

"Ready and—Action!" Ron calls.

"My motorcycle!" Philip says, sounding surprised and dismayed. "Somebody stole my motorcycle!"

"Cut," Ron calls when the scene is over. "That's good," he says. And then he adds, "Once more, please."

Most of Philip's scenes are with Ralph. Before the camera rolls, Ron shows Philip his eyeline, where the mouse will be. Then Philip goes over his part, and either the script woman or Ron takes Ralph's part. The mouse's "real" TV voice will be dubbed later; watching the film, an actor will synchronize the words with the movement of the mouse's mouth.

Philip is enchanted by the cute, lifelike puppet, and the scenes with it are great fun—at first. But as the days go by, he realizes that it is hard to react to a mechanical creature. And he finds himself saying his lines in the right tone of voice, but without feeling what Keith would feel.

"I don't see it in your face," Ron Underwood says, and they talk about the scene. Then Philip shuts out everything else, thinks about Keith, and feels the character.

Sometimes Ron helps him show an emotion. "You're sad, but you are not going to let yourself cry. The tears, though, are almost in your eyes." Each time, with Ron's coaching, Philip is able to get back into character, and the filming continues.

Philip enjoys the scenes with the actors who play his parents. But even more he enjoys the scenes with the bellhop, the only other person in the hotel who knows about Ralph. Ray Walston plays the part. Philip has seen Ray many times on TV and in the movies. Getting to act with him makes Philip feel like a real pro.

The two weeks seem to rush by. Soon it is the last day of filming, and the final scene is being shot. "And cut," Ron says at the end of the take. Then he raises an arm victoriously and adds, "Good. Great. It's in the can!"

Soon cast and crew are gathered in an outside room. There's cake and punch. Everyone is saying good-bye to everyone else, and Ron thanks Philip for having done a terrific job. Philip is pleased that Ron liked his performance, but he suddenly feels a little sad.

"I wish it wasn't over," Philip tells his mom as they drive home. "I wish it was the first day and we were just arriving. It was so exciting."

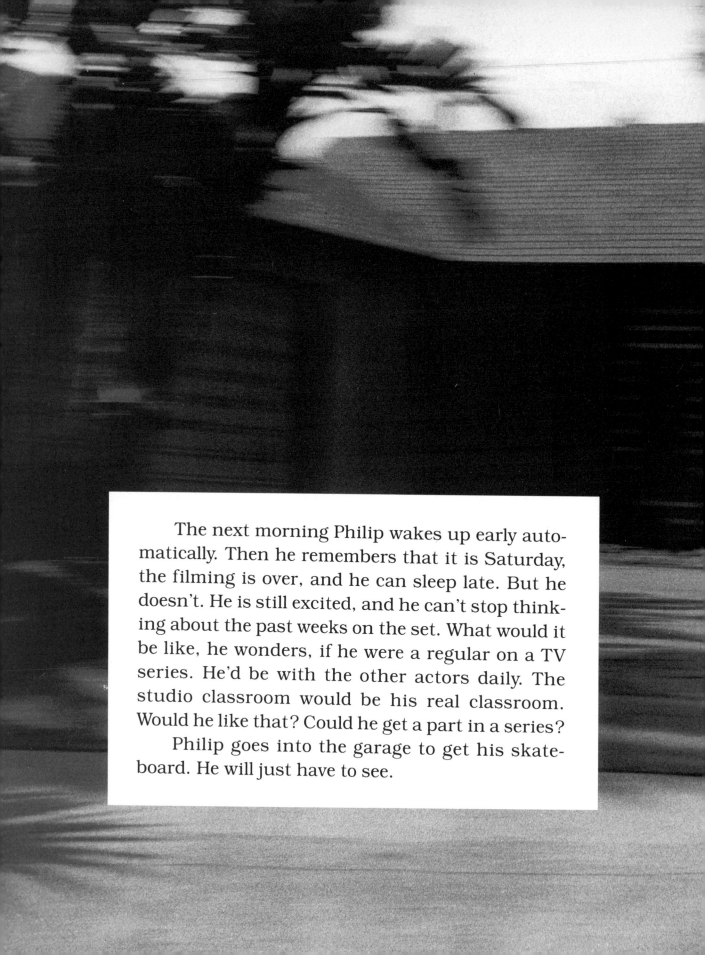

The next morning Philip wakes up early automatically. Then he remembers that it is Saturday, the filming is over, and he can sleep late. But he doesn't. He is still excited, and he can't stop thinking about the past weeks on the set. What would it be like, he wonders, if he were a regular on a TV series. He'd be with the other actors daily. The studio classroom would be his real classroom. Would he like that? Could he get a part in a series?

Philip goes into the garage to get his skateboard. He will just have to see.

ACKNOWLEDGMENTS

Throughout the months spent on this project, many people kindly opened doors for us so we might follow and observe our subject, Philip Waller. We are particularly indebted to Churchill Films and the creators of the TV special *The Mouse and the Motorcycle*— George McQuilkin, executive producer; John Matthews, producer and director of animation; Ron Underwood, director—for their generous cooperation and assistance. Thank you.

For their varied and valuable contributions we also thank: Richard Fish; Penelope Casadesus of Grey Advertising; Kelly of Kelly Casting; Diane Hardin, Nora Eckstein, and Stefan Haves of Young Actors Space; Virginia Lee Taylor, and Joann Damiani of Le Petit Repertory Theatre; Vivian Hollander and Estelle Hertzberg of Twentieth Century Artists, Inc.; and Don Jim.

A sincere thanks to Philip Waller and his parents, Kathy and Howard, as well as his sisters, Maria and Nicole, for their enthusiasm for this project and their unflagging cooperation. We would also like to take this opportunity to thank our editor, Ann Troy, for her thoughtful, insightful assistance.